How to Start an Orphanage in Africa

A Guide to a Non-Profit Organisation

Lucy Sabiiti

Founder of Blessed Hill Children's Centre

Copyright © 2020 Lucy Sabiiti

All rights reserved. No part of this publication may be reproduced, distributed, or transmitted in any form or by any means, including photocopying, recording, or any other electronic or mechanical methods, without the prior written permission of the publisher, except in the case of brief quotations embodied in critical reviews and certain other noncommercial uses permitted by copyright law. For permission, write to the publisher at:

Greatness University Publishers
London, UK
www.greatnessuniversity.co.uk

ISBN: 978-1-913164-73-7
ISBN-13: 978-1-913164-73-7

Dedication

To My darling late husband, Mr. Eric Sabiiti Jasi RIP, with whom we started the journey of setting up an orphanage. To all my children and their families, thank you all for the unconditional love, guidance, and mentorship to me even when things were hard, you believed in me. You have been the wind beneath my wings. I could think of no greater family than mine to have been honoured by God to be a part of.

How to Start an Orphanage

CONTENTS

Acknowledgments	vii
Foreword by Sir Clyde Rivers	ix
Preface	x
Introduction	15
My Story	19
Start an Orphanage?	31
Publicise Your Orphanage	43
International Development	47
Where do I get kids from?	53
Useful Information	61
Not Sure to Start an Orphanage?	67
Resource Mobilisation for an Orphanage	71
Corporate Governance	77
The Entrepreneurial Structure	83
Enterprise Risk Management	93
A Humanitarian	103
Strategic Organisation Development	107
Conclusion	111
About the Author	115

Acknowledgements

I acknowledge that God alone gets the Glory for this book and the establishment of Blessed Hill Children's center, an Orphanage in Uganda.

I could never speak of success and not acknowledge all the great men and women that are associated with me as sponsors and stood with me and the orphans for years. I am forever grateful to you and will forever hold you close to my heart and uplift you in my prayers.

I also acknowledge the cooperation and support I have received through many individuals. First and foremost, my sincere thanks to my son in law Prof. Patrick Businge for his time, support, encouragement, and expertise to make this book. Thanks to my mentor Ambassador Sir Clyde Rivers for all the support.

To all my children , Dr. Julian Businge, Mrs. Sheila Bagaya Burum, Mrs.Angella Sabiiti Batebe -you truly were my backbone after you finished your studies at university and we spent lots of sleepless nights together and cried together when things went well and bad too, my baby girl Mrs. Mary Sabiiti Roche,Mr. Jack Mutegeki, Mrs. Barbra Sabiiti Waako, Ms June

Lydia, to all their spouses, I thank God for you.

To all my precious grandchildren, my adorable nieces and nephews, siblings, sponsors, volunteers, relatives, friends, my board of governors/ directors, Blessed Hill staff, management, my beautiful children at Blessed Hill center (past and present) and my pastors, to you all, your passion for life and unwavering support to me has awarded you all special places within my heart.

Am eternally indebted to you all for being a wonderful inspiration, encouragement, and support to me.

God Bless you all.

Foreword by Sir Clyde Rivers

Founder of iChange Nations

This book is authored by one of the legends in orphanage work on the African continent. Mrs. Lucy Sabiiti is a forerunner and a leading voice in this field. What I like about her book is that she teaches you how to start, scale and sustain an orphanage in real-time.

She has done this work for many years in the right way. She has turned children lives around and helped them to rewrite their future. This amazing woman continues to do what others fear to do. I am proud to call her the Champion for the African Child. I'm truly humbled to write this foreword for a true champion. I therefore invite you to read this book and be transformed by its message.

Preface

Mrs. Lucy Sabiiti

Founder of Blessed Hill Children's Centre

How to Start an Orphanage

I am a Ugandan, born in 1957, my parents are, my late mother, Ruth Kajobe Abwooli RIP, dad, late Mr Bishari Abooki RIP. I grew up in a big lovely family of 15 children. Am a widow with a purpose and desire to help children with no parents or guardians and give them a better life and a future. I lost my job back in 2004, it's at this point that life was very difficult but I didn't allow my dream to contribute positively to the lives of children in need die. I always want to be able to serve others and be a blessing.

I am writing this book with you in mind:

- People who have a desire to do humanitarian work in Africa for example starting an orphanage and manage it effectively.
- Fellow Africans, or Africanist people, but only those who are serious about creating development in Africa and revolutionizing life for others in Africa.
- An African parent or guardian in the diaspora who is looking for some insights on how to help others in need especially the orphan child.
- Young leaders seeking to make a difference in Africa.
- An individual curious about the disadvantaged.

- A friend of Africa, that is anyone who is genuinely involved in helping people and communities across Africa.

This book is to share a few tips, skills and knowledge that I have acquired from starting an orphanage with limited funds and God connecting me to destiny helpers, honestly I wouldn't have made it on my own, it's taken so many people in different departments to make it come together beautifully. There are steps to follow legally for all the people that would like to do humanitarian nonprofit work in Africa one day.

Since the first day of setting up my orphanage called Blessed hill children's center, it houses a lot of children without parents who have received a place called home, they are also supported morally, emotionally, mentally, spiritually, physically and given education. Many have gone on to be successful in life and have a positive impact to the community they live in.

Are you eager to contribute to the work of the international humanitarian support?

It is a fulfilling world as the joy of helping someone else especially a vulnerable child is a game changer. I remember Oprah Winfrey saying on her show, "life is not about how much money and assets you live when your gone but it is about how many lives that you have touched in your lifetime." This is your chance and time to help someone else. It can be challenging on one hand and on another hand yet so rewarding in so many ways and that is why am sharing some knowledge.

How to Start an Orphanage

Introduction

How to Start an Orphanage

By now you might have heard the word orphanage and maybe see people starting an orphanage or non-profit in Africa. You will read real stories that would encourage you and increase your faith. However, before we go into details, I would like to define an orphanage.

What is an Orphanage?

An Orphanage is a residential institution devoted to the care of orphans. They are children whose natural parents are deceased or otherwise unable or unwilling to care for them.

Natural parents, and sometimes natural grandparents,

are legally responsible for supporting children, but in the absence of these or other relatives willing to care for the children, they become a ward of the state, and orphanages are one way of providing for their care, housing and education.

It is frequently used to describe institutions or organisations in Africa, where it is a more accurate term, since the word orphan has a different definition in international adoption, some may refer to it as fostering or residential care for children.

Although many people presume that most children who live in orphanages are orphans, this is often not the case with four out of five children in orphanages having at least one living parent and most having some extended family.

A lot of us ask questions like:

- o I am a foreigner, am I allowed to serve?
- o What is the first step in starting a non-profit?
- o How much does it cost to start a non-profit?
- o Who will be against me?
- o What type of opposition should I expect?
- o What if I work a day job and run the orphanage at the same time?
- o How can I get the children for the orphanage?

How to Start an Orphanage

- What is required to sustain an orphanage?
- Where does the official process of starting an orphanage begin?
- Do you have any other useful information about starting a non-profit?

All these questions as you continue reading this book will be answered.

My Story

How to Start an Orphanage

Most of the children who I started with in my care, aside from my immediate family, are the children who came from a region or area that was facing some problems during that time. In the 1990s, the Allied Democratic Forces (ADF) rebels terrorized the Rwenzori region in the districts of Kasese, Bundibugyo and Kabarole found in Uganda for over a decade.

The Allied Defence Forces (ADF) and tribal clashes in the Rwenzori region and DR Congo has left behind hundreds of orphans. So have the continuous landslides in Bugisu sub-region and floods.

Most of these orphans commonly drop out of school when the tragedy falls and escape to the city of Kampala, the capital of Uganda. Its where they hope to begin a new life through approaching voluntary organizations, becoming house helpers, looking for lost relatives, some become beggars on the street and others seek for well-wishers. Not all of them are that lucky to eventually find help.

Back in 1990, after losing some of my brothers to the deadliest epidemic AIDS, I had to take full responsibility for their children (my nieces and nephews) as well as for my own 7 children. It was not an easy journey but as a parent, I never gave up.

How to Start an Orphanage

Seeing a lot of children in my neighborhood that are orphaned, neglected, and abandoned my heart was moved to take care of some of them, and I decided to be a mother to those children. I chose to take them in and house them in a rented building living with a matron onsite which I later registered as an orphanage school.

My husband suggested that we hire teachers to educate these children to study from home, as it would have been extremely expensive to pay for each child's fees in public schools. When my dear husband died, life became complicated for both me and my children. I lost my job and could no longer pay the rent on the orphanage. At the end of our rent agreement, my landlord refused to renew the contract and we were forced to close the orphanage school I had started with. It was such an emotional time, but I had nowhere else to take the children and I had to part ways with some of them and stayed with over 25 in my home until I found help.

Losing my husband in December 2007 was the worst thing that happened to my family. He was lovely, hardworking and he treated me like a Queen in my palace. He did so many things like, he would take care of the children as his own, plan, advise me and support me in every way possible. The day he died, I felt like they should bury me too so I can go with him. I didn't feel any more strength and courage to move on in life without him. But with God, everything is possible, for he picked me up.

I thank God for raising an army of people starting with my own children, relatives, friends, volunteers, sponsors, pastors, to mention but a few from around the world that stood by me till today. This has enabled me to stand strong in the gap and be a blessing to the precious children in my care. When I look back, it was not easy, but it was worth it and I decided to move forward. We lead by example, never to give up, just keep the faith in God that all things are working together for good.

How to Start an Orphanage

One day while in my local church, we had visitors from England who asked women to write out their dream projects or proposals so that a few would be successful and be funded for the project and by God's grace, mine was successful, that was my turning point when I started receiving help, little by little until I managed to organize myself and rented another piece of land on which I built a temporary structure for the children and it was a fresh start in 2008.

2011 was a difficult year for us with lot of misfortunes. We had a case of a sick child who died so quickly after falling sick; The children of our landlord (the landlord died in 2010), they evicted us from their property as they wished to develop the site and the orphans were left homeless again. Some of the sponsorship I was receiving then was for 5 children maximum. Funding was not enough at that time, I struggled with the children in my home. I cried to God who alone has the power to change any situation and change our story.

Our miracle delayed but God did not deny us our breakthrough and in 2013, we were blessed with a sponsor from UK, Mr. Aughton Ainsworth. He purchased a 3-acre piece of land for us in Mityana and he has continued to be our support. The children were sent to boarding school whilst the orphanage school was being built and in January 2015 we finally moved into the new home for the children. This is one of the greatest miracles and testimony in my life and that of the children.

This journey has not been an easy one, but it is worth taking a leap of faith to see children getting a second chance to a better life. I almost gave up because the burden was too heavy for me, but nothing is impossible with God. God gave me courage and more wisdom. God has been good, and I believe that he will continue to be gracious.

Interview in the Ugandan Daily Newspaper

Daily monitor newspaper on October 10 2016, reported:

From her savings as a cashier at Kampala City Council, Sabiiti rented a house, on Salaama Road in Makindye where she was able to take care of about 30 children. But in 2007, the cruel hand of death, snatched her husband, a sales manager at Gulf Air. "This left her the burden of paying the teachers single-handedly, feeding and clothing the orphans. But I had to carry on," she says.

How to Start an Orphanage

However, more problems were yet to come. "My landlady also fell sick and died, leaving behind children who were not interested in the extension of the rent contract with us. We were thrown out of the house and I had no choice but to send back some of the orphans to the communities where I had picked them from and stayed with some children in my home who had nowhere else to go."

How to Start an Orphanage

Sabiiti was at one time arrested by police on accusations that she was dealing in child trafficking. "I cried. I knew I was doing the right thing. I was released and I continued building my capacity." She said.

One day a visiting pastor from UK came to my local church, known as Pastor Adrian, said he could get some sponsors for the orphans," narrates Sabiiti with a smile.

Indeed, Pastor Adrian got us the sponsor who bought land to build a permanent home in Mityana .A small town known as Kikonge-Kyengeze for the children.

In late 2013 Aughton Ainsworth purchased acres of land for us. Today, the school attracts orphans from as far as Mbale and Fort Portal, etc. There are over 200 completely parentless children from diverse backgrounds.

Majority of people from distant areas get to know about the project through churches especially during conferences in which the pastors and the congregations are introduced to the project.

Benefiting the Vicinity

The community has benefited so much from the project in terms of employment opportunities as most of the teachers employed by Blessed Hill are from the community.

"The project has not only provided affordable education services for the orphans and extend to the community but also provided a ready market for the community's commodities like food,(matooke or green bananas, beans, vegetables), a medical center where children who are sick can go, as we don't have our own facilities yet"

The school is still in the process of getting their own UNEB center number although they are fully registered. Finalists on primary level P.7 candidates currently sit from competent neighboring schools and our performance has continuously been promising.

Unlike many other primary schools and orphanages in the country, "What makes our project different from other projects offering the same service is that the project offers these young boys and girls simple life skills like knitting, jewelry making, art and craft, music and entertainment, through engaging them in vocational life skills during evening class and on some weekends.

Our dream for a vocation school is big hoping to become a university one day, but it doesn't stop us from starting small. The most tasking challenge is the lack of adequate accommodation, medical facilities since we are still constructing other blocks, for different age groups. We do not want to mix them all up. Every support, idea etc. is always welcome. We never stop learning and listening in order to grow and benefit others.

How to Start an Orphanage

Blessed Hill Children's Centre

Kikonge Kyengeza along Mityana Road
P.O. BOX 35385 Kampala, Uganda

Blessed Hill Children Centre is a registered NGO Christian based organization whose goal is to support, educate, feed and house orphaned, abandoned, and rejected children for a positive social change.

Am a mother to many nations. It has taken having faith in God to bring me divine helpers from all over the world to help me buy acres of land, setup the school professionally, I have a great management team of day to day affairs.

All the children need a safe place to be taken care of, they need to go to school, eat, and be clothed, medical etc. God opened a way, some of the children have managed to make it through to University, and then they come back and give me a helping hand.

How to Start an Orphanage

Start an Orphanage?

How to Start an Orphanage

Have you ever felt that you would like to be a humanitarian one day? The heart usually will be willing, and the mind will be hesitant to take the risk of starting the humanitarian project. I mean the feeling of worry and anxiety. Am speaking from experience. Here in Africa we have seen people hurt poor people in some of the following ways.

we get stuck on relief and rehabilitation, and never move on to development. Relief and rehabilitation are necessary parts of a recovery plan for all human beings who have faced adversity. But they can hurt communities when they don't take another step to empower the people to have life skills that will make them self-sufficient than relying on international aid alone. Always work with the charities to promote development which brings self-sustainability, create partnerships, friendships that last a lifetime and development starts here. The very people who have been assisted out of a problem will go on to help others too around the world.

We must change the way we talk and think about Africa.eg the worse the children look; the more money they can make from rich western countries. Prevent commercializing the orphans.

How to Start an Orphanage

The stereotype of African people as helpless and dependent on Western help is one that has been built by decades of well-meaning but arguably dangerous charity advertisements in the West. Bombarded by images of sad, dirty children with eyes that call you to urgently donate money, it is no surprise that this is a common belief. Anybody can be in a disadvantaged position.

Not everybody in Africa is sick. Furthermore, we should treat those who do suffer from HIV, or any other illness, the way we would want to be treated - with dignity and respect.

African communities are advertised as helpless, hopeless, and inadequate thereby have an alleviation system. Western media has it that they are afraid of poor people in Africa making decisions with the money they send, so they budget it for them and don't give accountability.

In other words, what you think is the right road may lead to death. The different negative opinions about Africa from different people can block someone else from being a blessing. We all matter and are one human race of brothers and sisters. We should not allow this to cause us to be too afraid to serve the poor. God has not given us a Spirit of fear, but of love, power, and of a sound mind.

There is a proverb that says, "It is not good to have zeal without knowledge, nor to be hasty and miss the way." (Prov. 19:2).

An orphanage is a non-profit organization. It should not be set up with the intention of making money. An orphanage is a home where children with no known or responsible guardians willing to take care of them are kept. The orphanage helps to provide a family-like environment for these children. Orphanages also play major roles in nurturing and mentoring children; we have received children as young as 6 months.

Before starting up, I recommend every interested party to prepare themselves by doing the following:

Get Professional Training

Acquiring and developing the skill of caring for others is important if you intend to be successful.

Participation in training courses will help to further the skills that you need to effectively run the orphanage. I and my team, offer 1 to 1 coaching or group training, make sure to contact us if interested.

Volunteer in an Orphanage

Volunteering helps give you the experience of how an orphanage is run on a day to day basis. If you volunteer in a reputable orphanage, you will learn from the workings of the best. Contact us know if interested in working with us.

Adequate Research

Research as much as possible on how to start an orphanage in the country, town etc. Focus on areas like legal requirements, children and infant care, child psychology, non-profit fundraising, they usually have a lot of information that can help you make a decision etc.

After doing the required work, it is time to put the infrastructure on the ground. Even though you don't have enough money, start from your own home with a few children.

Create a proposal

This will give you compass direction on what and where to begin from in terms of establishing the actual structural orphanage especially if you already live in Africa. It can be tempting to craft a proposal to start an orphanage in a location where orphans are desperately in need of care, but this is easier said than done.

Many countries do not allow foreigners to operate an orphanage, so you will likely need to seek residency or citizenship to begin the process and start an orphanage.

Instead of opening an orphanage in Africa, Asia or another part of the world, it is more feasible to partner with an already established orphanage in the area where you want to make an impact.

Try spending a month or two volunteering in the orphanage before making a permanent move to ensure it is the right fit for you. Alternatively, an already established organization could create a proposal to start an orphanage for you and then provide the means for you to reside on-site and care for the children.

There are so many countries in Africa and their laws regarding starting an orphanage may vary from country to county. Ask the respective countries embassy or consulate if can get a hold of them or try some NGO's consultants or lawyers.

Raising Capital

Before going into this, you need to be very clear as to how you intend to raise the capital for starting and running it. If you don't, you have to map out a plan as to how you intend to raise funds.

It is a common mistake to believe that your orphanage will begin to generate funds to run itself from the onset. Slowly but steadily, with publicity and the proper use of social media, your orphanage will thrive with donations. Orphanages are expensive sometimes and lack sustainability, if not planned well in advance. It costs not less than $3,000/year per child in an orphanage, on average.

Location

In selecting a location for your orphanage, go for clean, quiet, and serene environments. Do not forget that the end goal is to raise children there, so it is important that the environment be conducive. It is also important that the orphanage be visible and accessible to donors. The orphanage should also be in a place with room for expansion.

The building type needed for an orphanage is largely dependent on the number of children that you intend to accommodate at any given time. If there is room enough for every child to play and learn.

At a minimum, the children should have a sleeping area, eating area, play area and study area for the more matured ones among them. Have it in mind that before you will be allowed to register your orphanage, there some stringent requirements that must be met with respect to the location.

Get Registered

The setting up and running of orphanages is strictly regulated by the government. It is illegal, even criminal offence to start an orphanage in Uganda or another African country without first going through the necessary registration process.

The registration processes and the penalty for defaulters are captured in the Child Rights Act. In Uganda, the Non-Governmental Organizations are regulated by the Non-Governmental Organizations Registration Act Cap 113 as amended in 2006. The Act governs the registration, management and governance of Non-Governmental Organizations.

It is important that you register. First You need the following in Uganda, and I believe somehow similar to other African nations.

How to Start an Orphanage

- It is a legal requirement that your first incorporate a company limited by guarantee before registering as an NGO, therefore you will need the following.
- Reservation of a name, two copies of the Article and Memorandum of Association, fill the application form for registration, accompanied by Forms 18 (notice of situation of registered office) & 20 (particulars of Directors), pay registration fees in the bank, attach all above documents and submit to Uganda Registration Service Bureau (URSB).
- Within 2-3 days you will be issued with a Certificate of Incorporation. Allowing you to operate as a Company Limited by Guarantee.

The next step is to register as an NGO. You need:

- A letter of recommendation written by Local Council One Chairperson (LC I).
- Written recommendation of two sureties or recommenders who should each write separately recommending the organization
- A work plan of its activities to be carried out for the first year of the term of operation. The activities or work plan for the one year should have budget

How to Start an Orphanage

- Two copies of the Constitution or by By-Laws or Rules and should have a provision in it specifying the purposes for which the funds are to be utilized
- An Organizational Chart/Administrative chart showing its leadership.
- Write a letter to the Secretary NGO Board specifying the area of their operation. This is what will be printed on the permit once granted
- Reserve its name with the Registrar General's Office at the Ministry of Justice or attach a copy of reservation of name of the company Limited by Guarantee from URSB.
- Copies of identification documents for at least two founders.
- Recommendation from the line ministry recommending you work as an NGO, e.g. Ministry of Education.
- Minutes and resolution by directors allowing to register as an NGO.
- An application to NGO Board signed by two directors.
- Where you have fulfilled with all the requirements, you will be issued with a

Certificate of Registration, and a Permit to operate within that country for a given period usually two to five years.

A Non-Profit Business Management Plan

It is important to have a plan as to how you intend to run your orphanage. This plan should include things like the number of personnel, criteria for accepting children, strategy on fundraising, and other important aspects of the project.

How to Start an Orphanage

How to Start an Orphanage

Publicise Your Orphanage

After completing the set-up stage, the next thing in the list is to publicize, create an online presence, build trust. Ensure that you publicize your orphanage. It enables you to attract donors and patrons to your orphanage. Publicity can take various forms such as flyers, social media, posters, and adverts.

Create an Online Presence

Creating a website for your orphanage will give you even more exposure. There are some international bodies, agencies, and individuals who adopt orphanages.

This will help to strengthen the financial base of your orphanage. There is an orphanage in Uganda called Watoto, led by a prominent pastor in Kampala, Children travel all around the world doing music concerts and drama, this helps them raise funding. Am so proud of them and pray we will follow suit too one day.

Build Trust

This is not a one-day activity, we all must listen to each other as the most important factor to building integrity. A person trusts another when they feel that they can be vulnerable, and everything will be alright. You can build trust in your relationships with the children and all others in the organization if you are prepared to make the effort.

There are lots of orphanages scattered over major cities. Some have been found to be dubious. Stand out from the crowd by being honest and open in all your dealings. It is more a labor of love than profit.

Grants for Orphans

Seek funding through grants and corporate and individual donors. People who serve in orphanages abroad often find financial support from their religious institutions, while organizations that start them must make a full-time job of soliciting donations to help cover operational costs.

According to the website of the non-profit agency Cry of the Orphan, there are more than 13 million children worldwide who have lost both their mother and father. The site also reports that orphans are more prone to become victims of violence, exploitation and other injustices.

Children can become orphaned for various reasons including natural disasters and diseases. While orphans cannot take care of themselves, grants are available to help improve their quality of life.

How to Start an Orphanage

How to Start an Orphanage

International Development

How to Start an Orphanage

This is an idea how the western world deals with this issue concerning the orphan child and in Africa we could easily adopt too the ideas. There is a United States Agency for International Development, it is an agency that strives to work to protect children's rights, offers a Displaced Children and Orphans Fund. We need such agencies in Africa too.

Agencies that register with the United States Agency for International Development may be eligible to receive grants. Criteria for selection include programs that meet the needs of children who have been affected by war or separated from adult caregivers.

Programs that have the highest impact for children and focus on the physical and emotional needs of children while valuing religious and cultural practices are given priority.

Orphanage Fund

I have heard about this helping system in Europe but not personally used them. It's called The Associate Reformed Presbyterian Church in America. They give grant offers for financial assistance to organizations that provide projects for the physical, educational, emotional and spiritual care for orphans in a Christian setting. Grants are awarded of five years.

Adoption costs

In some countries, people prefer to adopt children into a family, which is even excellent. Show Hope, an organization that encourages the church to take care of orphans and to reduce the financial burden of adoption, offers $1 million a year in grants to help put orphans into Christian families.

Families with the greatest financial need are given the highest priority for adoption grants. The number and financial amount of grants depends on the amount of funds available.

God created families and he intends for us to grow up in them. They encourage to invest in solutions that allow for orphans and vulnerable children to be raised in loving safe environments and that's why in our orphanage we have matrons who are like mothers to the children and can report to me in case of any problem.

The hardest thing by far is getting the initial start-up costs. Obviously, this number changes dramatically depending on what you want to do, starting cash for an orphanage of around 10-30 kids this is assuming you had the building already or willing to start small shouldn't be more than around US$10,000 -$30,000 to get completely registered and equipped.

No matter where you are from, if you're receiving large sums of money while in Africa, you'll need to abide by African laws governing that particular country you are receiving from. They are put in place to protect both your money and the interests of the government.

For people receiving money into Africa legally need the following.

Choose from several different methods to transfer money from foreign countries. Depending on where you are located and the amount you want to send, you may choose to work with a bank to write a check or do a wire transfer. You can also use a remittance service to transfer money. For large sums of money, use a foreign exchange service.

There are many people who think that just because you are running an NGO you must be incredibly rich. Generally, though, it is quite the opposite. Most of our members would personally have less than $200 in their bank accounts and their only real "assets" are their motorcycles or scooters. It's about the helping heart to serve others.

Many businesses that we deal with are sympathetic to our cause, they give us great discounts and become some of our most active supporters. Sometimes you also have to be aware of religious and political agendas, these both can affect the way people treat you and your organization.

This applies from the smallest situations like people donating to your cause right up to Government Offices. We don't know why people act this way; we should all be concerned about the needy no matter what religion is involved.

Keeping on working while you run the orphanage is not impossible. It all depends on:

How to Start an Orphanage

- How many kids do you have?
- How many employees do you have?
- Whether or not you can get assistance from any other NGO's (i.e. finance/volunteers)

Our suggestion would be to start out VERY small. No more than 2-4 kids. Try it for a year or two; work out the boundaries you need to set in your life between work and the orphanage: your old family and your new family.

There are loads of stresses & lifestyle changes that come with having a regular child let alone 2-4 children who might have spent anywhere up to 15 years living on the streets. Do not rush into anything as sustainability is what is important. It is better to help 1 orphan for their whole life than 1000 orphans without the proper care.

How to Start an Orphanage

Where do I get kids from?

Many of our children are brought here by their family members when a parent dies or next of kin. Some are brought by the police. Some are brought by the Human Rights Association, Welfare Department or local council or village chiefs, social workers.

We do not take any children without the written permission of the District Magistrate or Welfare Department. Our suggestion would be to get your organization connected with the following:

- Local Police, Local councils, Government Offices, Local village chiefs etc.
- Human Rights Association
- Any NGO's operating in your area that have similar goals
- Local press / journalists

At the very least write a letter to each category above and post via Registered Mail (as then they won't just think it is junk mail). A week or two later you could visit their offices in person (just to let them see that you are serious). It is good to have your goals/vision draw up on paper.

What is required to sustain an orphanage?

This is certainly not a complete list but here are a few things that are particularly important in regard to sustainability: The biggest need will always be money. Don't kid yourself; you are going to need a lot of it, especially as your orphanage grows in size.

Foreign or domestic support can help in this regard, but it is a good idea to look at sustaining your project through other areas. We need funds for our bores, solar power, greenhouses, (saves on the bill expenses and maintenance) sheds, animals, seedlings, and farm equipment to allow us to begin food production as soon as possible.

Running a Primary School or Kindergarten is a great example and one that has worked well for our organization. We invite normal children with parents who can afford school fees from the community to study in our school and pay a fee.

As the children increase, you will find that you/your family are not able to "do it alone" and you will need help. Good people are hard to find, especially when you need them to work for cheap! Start looking for help long before you need it.

A good website that clearly states your goals/purposes. This really does make a difference. These days everyone uses the net, you can access it on your phone! It is important to get your name out there.

Where does the official process of starting an orphanage begin?

Here are a few of the really important first steps, they are not in any specific order, but should all be completed before you take in any children.

Set a location

Acquire a piece of property to base the organization immediately if possible, eventually have it registered in the name of the organization or find someone willing to give a legal lease for long term (the minimum is something like 10-15 years).

Get Letters of Support

Get as many letters of support as you can, as fast as you can, from local businesses, politicians, dignitaries, foreign businesses, local chiefs/village heads, individuals, etc. These will all help to avoid delays/problems in your registration/setup process.

A Letter of Support

This can be as simple as a person writing "I am in support of the work that …. is proposing in the …. area. If you are able to support it. We would appreciate it.

Signed

You can send these letters off, i.e. start with the smaller people/businesses in your region and use a collection of the letters approving from them to get funding out of people holding higher positions even in government.

Get Your Society Registered

A society is a group of people with a common goal and come together to achieve that goal. Combining resources to achieve a common goal for example, if we intend to build a house for the children in a certain area and have community development.

Register the organization as a Society if the directors agree as an option to work together in big numbers. This is done through your local Registrar of Societies), if you need help finding them ask at your local government office i.e. ask a lawyer there at the courts.

For this you will need a Board of Directors, and a few other things. You can ask at the Registrars of Societies office about the process for this, requirements are different in each city or country.

Get Your Orphanage Registered

All orphanages and children's homes in Africa must be registered under a government approved agency.

Register with the Income Tax Department.

Depending on which country, you will need to Register of your society for a PAN number (Permanent Account Number) is essential. After this you can ask at your local tax office about applying for the "tax-free" status known as 12A Registration.

In Uganda, the NGO is a required to file returns to the URA (Uganda Revenue Authority) every year showing income and expenditure, but corporate tax is not charged because you are not making any profits.

If you want people who donate to you from within Africa to be able to claim the donation as "tax deductible" then you will need 80G Registration; the application process for this is complicated and you will definitely need the help of a registered Chartered Accountant.

Get an Accountant

It's a good idea to have a permanent accountant - either contracted or on your payroll. Accountability is essential for any organization to survive. Audited financial reports by a Chartered Accountant are a legal requirement for NGO's operating in Africa.

Get a Solicitor

It's a good idea to have a permanent lawyer too. Lots of different documents will have to be drafted for your new organization such as a Memorandum of Association, applications for registration etc. and it is best to have a professional do this.

Start looking for funding

Finding funding is a difficult thing but if you register as a Society which means a group of people with one vision come together with their resources and get registration you can apply for grants from businesses and other NGO's. Corporate Social Responsibility programs are a great place to start.

How to Start an Orphanage

How to Start an Orphanage

Useful Information

How to Start an Orphanage

There are some great books out there on the subject of starting an NGO. One of the books that our team found useful was called "Legal Handbook for Christian Services in Africa" which should be available from decent Christian Bookstores in Africa Even if you're not a Christian there is a lot of relevant information in there for non-profits and especially those involving foreigners/foreign aid.

Different laws work in different in Africa. There are also some laws that you absolutely need to be aware of, it is good to have these books on hand most can be bought online through the Eastern Book Company:

- Societies Registration Act
- Foreign Contribution Regulation Act
- Income Tax Act
- Juvenile Justice (Care and Protection of Children) Act

Some others that are nice to know too:

- The Constitution of Africa
- Payment of Wages Act
- The Charitable & Religious Trusts Act
- Basic Education Act

How to Start an Orphanage

- Right to Information Act
- Foreigners Registration Act
- The Minimum Wages Act.

Everywhere I go to speak about the issues of orphans around the world, inevitably a question comes up from a well-meaning individual: "How do I start an orphanage?"

I smile politely - knowing that they've typically not thought through all of the implications - and I ask some probing questions:

- What area of the world are you considering?
- What is the country? What city?
- What are the major issues facing children in that area?
- Do you have a building?
- The country laws concerning orphans.

Usually I don't get past question number one. The person in question hasn't thought through any of the issues. Typically, they say they feel that they are called to go help orphans.

I love the calling, but hate the lack of thought behind it. So, before you quit your job, sell your home, your possessions and move off to the far reaches of the world, let's add in some clarity and thought. You do not have to travel to the other side of the world to help orphans.

Are you good at fundraising or can you speak to large audiences with passion and conviction? Then let me suggest you find an orphan organization that you can believe in and passionately give to and help them raise support. There are many good organizations out there, step in and be an advocate for children within your own community.

You Should Visit Orphans

Despite some bad press around the world and the few people visiting Africa that are focused entrepreneurs in other countries, there are some orphanages and orphan focused programs in Africa that could use your help.

There are some benefits to both the visited and the visitor, including:

Benefits to the Orphanage

The staff are often working many late hours to care for the children. Even taking the children on an outing or taking the time to play with them allow the staff a much-needed break.

Teams of visitors often bring specific individuals who can help supplement the education of the children. Many times, in our orphanage, visitors usually teach English to children and adults to help supplement their education.

I've heard about an organization, it's one of the Orphan World Relief programs in America that provides training for teenagers who have graduated from the state-run orphanage system. This is so awesome and would be great for such organisations to extend to Africa.

New capabilities at an orphanage. Orphanages and programs supporting at-risk children can often become more self-sufficient. Teams of visitors can bring new ventures to benefit the staff and the children.

Over the years I've seen all manner of new offerings including cattle and chicken farm; vegetable gardens; goat farm; and, sewing machines to start a small sewing business. It's a fantastic Boost to the economy. Successful orphanages become a part of the community.

Benefits to the visitor

It is a life changing program that makes us appreciate Gods' creation. While not everyone who visits an orphan program will be forever changed, others are changed by the visit and spend part of their time advocating or fundraising for well run programs.

You become globally aware of what happens by witness true stories. Some people are hindered by not looking beyond their own borders. There's a great benefit to seeing the world, any part of the world and realizing that there's not always "one right way" to live. Plus, we get a chance to see our own world through the eyes of others.

You learn to live with less resources. The poorest of our people have more than most of the world. Sometimes it helps to see that. Some people have options on whatever they want to eat on a daily basis and take it for granted and don't get to understand that it's a privilege that some children don't have but you could be a solution to them.

Not sure to start an orphanage?

How to Start an Orphanage

Start small. Take it in small chunks and go from there moving forward and it is going to take time and eventually all come together for good.

Find a program in an African country that is professionally managed. The one you can get behind and go visit them for a few weeks or months. We at Blessed Hill are ready to welcome you in Uganda, just send us an email and we can arrange.

If you are not yet sure after spending some time with them, but deep in your heart ,you still feel called to start an orphanage, contact another orphanage in a different area before you settle to partner with one, do more than observe, ask to shadow the staff members.

Relocate for a longer period 6 months to a year to live with the children and see their daily routines. Pay your own way and work beside the orphanage every day, through the sickness, the broken bones, the temper tantrums, the kids being adopted out, it's a learning process.

Learn the local codes and rules and regulations. You need to find out the laws governing you being in that country and the orphanage too. Learn everything you can.

How to Start an Orphanage

Consider what's best. Rather than opening up another orphanage, help the one you're working with expand so that they can grow and take on more children if there's a need in that community.

Some people prefer partnerships, it's not to create something new or start from scratch but join in the work already being done. You might be able to save yourself many headaches.

Perhaps you've got skills that the program you're supporting is in desperate need of, you could be that person to really enhance the lives of children in a significant and life-long way.

Starting something new sounds glamorous... until you have to do it. Come alongside a group and enhance them and help them grow.

Looking for a place to visit, let me recommend a wonderful nonprofit organization and that is Blessed Hill, contact us through email or social media

Our orphanage is a well-run organization that partners with amazing programs around the globe supporting orphans and at-risk kids. Want to donate directly to helping children, give monthly to Blessed Hill? You can make a difference in the lives of orphans by just giving a little.

How to Start an Orphanage

How to Start an Orphanage

Resource Mobilisation for an Orphanage

Increasing financial security is very vital. One option could be through grants and donations to fund the school.

Another way could be through self-generating services directed toward the public, selling promotional items in shops or the internet, fundraising, seek new corporate donors for monetary or in-kind support, hold events that would generate money for example concerts where you would charge minimal entry fees.

Form partnerships with groups. See if the national and local government has some programs that provide support. Look into investment holdings. One-time charity events with proceeds go to the school. In the interior of any orphanage, resource mobilization is one of the activities used to secure additional resources and make better use of the existing ones.

It is very critical to any orphanage prompting to them having donors supporting the children within this organization.

Each orphanage entails improvement to all their services and amendment of the environment that encompasses the orphaned and the workers. The funds make available a stronghold that harnesses the capability of the children thus promoting a good understanding

The well-being of the orphans within an orphanage is supported by community support groups, the government, and rich individuals. For the providence of such support, a good project proposal should be written and handed over to the seniors within the administration.

The type of support offered enhances a plan initiation and execution, the achievement of the proposed goals, and alignment of the orphanage activities to reach targets. Research has shown that the effective organizational management of orphanages is offered by individuals working within the care centers.

The role of the workers is to nurture the optimal well-being of orphans. Personnel governing the orphanage ought to offer education to these children and standardize all their daily activities. They should be experienced to stand firm with the visions and train the employees accordingly. This is to enhance a healthy and prosperous generation that comes out of the care of children.

Risk management exposure affects the ability to reach the stated objectives of an orphanage. Conferring to exploration the directors should stand in place to moderate compliance risks that are identified and address them accordingly.

This will help curb the emotional and behavioral problems of the orphans caused by exposure to neglect, abuse, and lack of parental care and guidance.

Project Management

This is the application of knowledge, skills, tools, and techniques to project activities to meet the project requirements.

It has always been practiced informally but began to emerge as a distinct profession in the mid-20th century. PMI's A Guide to the Project Management Body of Knowledge (PMBOK® Guide) identifies its recurring elements:

Project management processes fall into five groups:

1. Initiating
2. Planning
3. Executing
4. Monitoring and Controlling
5. Closing

Project management knowledge draws on ten areas:

1. Integration
2. Scope
3. Time
4. Cost
5. Quality
6. Procurement
7. Human resources
8. Communications
9. Risk management
10. Stakeholder management

All management is concerned with these, of course. But project management brings a unique focus shaped by the goals, resources and schedule of each project. The value of that focus is proved by the rapid, worldwide growth of project management:

- As a recognized and strategic organizational competence
- As a subject for training and education
- As a career path

Project Support Management

Project management support involves helping teams initiate, plan, execute, and complete work to achieve specific project goals.

People in these roles ensure projects are on target and that there is alignment across teams. They create tools and processes that help achieve project goals and manage any issues.

Corporate Governance

Corporate governance can be seen as having internal and external sources, where external corporate governance consists of mandatory and voluntary codes, reports and frameworks such as company law, rules and accounting and auditing standards.

Internal corporate governance is how such external governance is complied with and embedded within the culture and values of the organization and how sound governance is implemented and works in practice.

The corporate governance framework can play its part in providing a structure for governing the behavior of companies and their officers, but external rules, regulations, and codes of practice are not effective unless a climate of compliance within organizations is promoted to support such structures and mechanisms at all levels through such mechanisms as corporate and ethical codes of behavior and values.

There also needs to be a deeper culture embedded within the orphanage, recognizing the responsibilities and duties of management with regard to the legitimate rights of their stakeholders.

Effective corporate governance is about promoting this climate of transparency, skepticism and objectivity; by creating systems, procedures, and internal structures, aimed at complying with external requirements, but also pre-empting and dissuading anti-stakeholder behavior from deep within the organization.

Internal corporate governance (or the corporate culture) should therefore be instrumental in reducing the 'expectations gap' between the interests and motivations of the 'agent' and those of the 'principal'; thereby addressing the agency problem at all levels within the organization.

Organizational Management

Organizational Management is a combination of many components of leadership within a company. The actual structure of the company is utilized to gather information to analyze it. This analysis is then used to develop strategies that are then implemented and executed via meetings, training and promotion.

Purposes of Organizations

An organization is a group of people with a common purpose. The purpose is defined by the entity for which they work. In smaller businesses, such as partnerships and small companies, it is common for those who work for the organization to have created it, or to have had some part in creating it.

By contrast, larger organizations have to employ or involve more people, the majority of which will have little or no connection with the founders or owners.

The Development of Organisations

Organizations have been around for thousands of years. The mighty armies of Greece and Rome were organizations, and the Phoenician merchants who plied their trade across the oceans could not have run successful businesses without some organizational structure.

Whenever two or more people come together to pursue the same outcomes, we have an organization. Organizations exist because synergy can be achieved by combining human resources. Together, those in an organization can produce more than the sum total output of individuals working alone.

The industrial revolution of the eighteenth and nineteenth centuries brought a need for more systematic and formal consideration of how organizations should be configured. Adam Smith used the example of the division of labor in a pin factory to describe the benefits of specialization:

How to Start an Orphanage

'One man draws out the wire, another straight it, a third cuts it, a fourth points it, a fifth grinds it at the top for receiving the head: to make the head requires two or three distinct operations: to put it on is a particular business, to whiten the pins is another.

The important business of making a pin is, in this manner, divided into about eighteen distinct operations, which in some manufactories are all performed by distinct hands, though in others the same man will sometime perform two or three of them.' (The Wealth of Nations, 1776).

Generally, businesses start as small entities, and many remain so. Every country in the world has thousands of sole traders, many of which work alone and are able to make their living without involving others.

However, if the activities of the business grow, it eventually becomes necessary to utilize the labor of others. In family concerns, the trader may involve a spouse, children, or siblings, and this may not even require the creation of any contractual relationships.

Yet it does require some degree of organization. Who carries out which tasks? Does everybody do the same work or does everyone specialize? To what extent should everyone be able to carry out the tasks usually reserved for others?

How do we ensure that all work is done, but there is no wasteful duplication of effort? These questions can be addressed in a relatively informal manner in a small business where all control is in the hands of a single person.

However, the very same questions must be asked in the largest and most complex businesses, and for these the answers are less straightforward.

How to Start an Orphanage

The entrepreneurial Structure

The entrepreneurial structure is adopted by smaller businesses. It is simple, informal and very fluid, in that it may change on a day-to-day basis.

This structure is adopted by sole traders who employ others, some small partnerships and some small companies. Those who own and control the business take decisions on the work to be done, how it will be done and by whom.

It is quite common for employees to be expected to multitask and not to expect rigid job descriptions. Specialization may be possible, such as a family member dealing with bookkeeping, but that individual may also be required to carry out additional tasks, perhaps if there is no bookkeeping work to be done at certain times.

The entrepreneurial structure is perfect for many small businesses but is too informal and can even be chaotic once the level of business activity reaches a certain level.

Eventually, the entrepreneur must consider formalizing the roles that employees play and creating jobs with defined duties and responsibilities.

The Functional Structure

The functional structure is the most common organizational model. It is usually depicted as a triangle, with the chief executive officer at the top and reporting lines of others flowing vertically. The functional structure is formally depicted as an organization chart.

The duties of individuals are allocated according to the functions they perform. For example, a small company may have a production manager, finance manager, sales manager and IT manager reporting to the chief executive officer. Each of the functional managers is responsible for a department.

Many larger companies have general managers or assistant general managers responsible for groups of functions. For example, the General Manager (Marketing) may be responsible for advertising, public relations, merchandising and direct sales, and there may be a departmental manager responsible for each of these activities.

For each function, employees are grouped together to perform similar or complementary tasks. Just as the organization as a whole can be represented on an organization chart, so too can each department.

The functional structure is common to many

organizations, but different concepts can be deployed within it. For example:

The organization can be tall or flat: tall organizations have many levels (a long scalar chain), while flat organizations have fewer levels the organization may have many employees reporting to each manager, few employees reporting to each manager, or a combination of these.

This span of control will depend on many factors, including the nature of the work, variety of tasks performed, capabilities of employees and risk factors some organizations concentrate authority at the top of the management hierarchy, with key decisions taken by senior executives, while others empower subordinates, with greater discretion permitted further down the management chain: this relates to the concept of centralization and decentralization.

Functional Organization by Product

The functional model can be adapted for organizations that offer a range of products. Just as managers responsible for different products can report to the product manager, it is also possible for each product manager to have his or her own functional structure.

In this way, several functions are duplicated across the organization, as the manager responsible for each product may have their own production, sales, marketing, finance, and administration departments.

This organization structure is sometimes appropriate if the design, production, and marketing of each product is unique or significantly different to those for other products. This structure can also be suitable if products are distinctive brands

Functional organization by geographical region

Many organizations operate across different regions, or across international frontiers, so they may consider it to be appropriate to maintain separate functional structures in each location.

This approach is not appropriate to all geographically dispersed businesses but is suitable for organizations whose geographical locations have distinctive but contrasting characteristics.

Matrix Structure

The matrix structure evolved in companies that sought to overcome some of the rigidities of the functional organization structure. It was first deployed in the aerospace industry in the USA in the

1950s.

The most common application of the matrix structure is the creation of an extra layer of responsibilities across the traditional functional structure. As well has occupying a position in the organizational pyramid, which defines line relationships, employees have responsibilities to project managers. In this way, the employee may have two or even more managers.

Boundaryless Organizations

Traditionally, organizations bring people together in one or more physical locations in order to process inputs and create outputs, all within a formally defined structure. Advances in information communications technology have resulted in new approaches that have redefined where, when and how people work.

The most obvious evidence of this is the reduction in reliance on the 9.00am to 5.00pm working day, the emergence of flexible working arrangements and increases in work sharing and home working. Organizations have also adopted new ways of configuring relationships.

Virtual Organization

A virtual organization is one which operates primarily through electronic communications, taking advantage of the efficiencies made possible by information technology.

It removes many of the features of the working environment that were once taken for granted, such as bringing managers and staff together at a defined location.

People work together remotely, with little or no dependence on physical premises. Instead, communications take place through media such as emails, e-conferencing, extranet and intranet.

This virtual aspect of the operation sometimes extends to links with suppliers (upstream), and customers (downstream).

By extending the virtual concept to customer relationships, the dependence on retail premises and customer-facing staff is eliminated. Amazon is often cited as the first major virtual business in this respect.

The virtual organization model can be adopted wholly or in just certain parts of the business.

Hollow Organization

A hollow organization is one which relies heavily on outsourcing, enabling it to maintain low staffing levels while capitalizing on the competences of partner organizations.

The most common application of this model is where an organization identifies those competences that are core and must be retained. These are then kept in-house, while all non-core operations are contracted out.

The hollow organization must forge strong strategic links with trusted partners.

Modular Organization

A modular organization extends the hollow concept by breaking down production processes into modules. Production is outsourced, but each external organization is responsible for only one element of the process.

For example, in producing the Dreamliner aircraft, Boeing enters into contracts with many suppliers, each of which is responsible for one component or assembly. The outputs of these suppliers can then be integrated.

The modular organization is a more efficient, contemporary version of the model previously used by many car manufacturers, who often owned the subsidiaries which produced components that make up the final product.

The modular organization removes the need for complex ownership structures through holding companies and subsidiaries, and also creates forced efficiencies, as those responsible for each module have to compete with organizations in the same marketplace for their services.

Shared Services Organizations

The shared services organization is a medium through which defined services can be provided across the organization by a dedicated unit. This differs from outsourcing, in that the shared services provider is actually a part of the organization.

Shared services organizations reduce the level of duplication of tasks. For example, instead of each part of the organization employing human resources or information technology specialists, these services can be provided centrally, through a single team.

In this way, they can reduce costs significantly and also standardize the policies and processes across the

How to Start an Orphanage

business.

Enterprise Risk Management

This photo is with a visiting volunteer from the UK, we were given an idea of creating crafts and jewelry, then selling them locally and internationally to help support the children.

Enterprise Risk management, Is the practice of planning, coordinating, executing and handling the activities of an organization in order to minimize the impact of risk on investment and earnings?

ERM extends the approach to incorporate not only risks connected with unexpected losses, but also strategic, financial and operational risks.

- An ongoing process.
- Applied in strategy setting and across the enterprise.
- Designed to identify potential events that, if they occur, will affect the entity and to manage risk within its risk appetite.
- Provides reasonable assurance regarding the achievement of business objectives.

The Importance

Events over recent years have pointed to five realities that every CEO and board face:

1. The time may come – sooner than we may expect in the near future when the fundamentals of the business are about to change. Risk management is about securing "early mover" positioning in the marketplace.

Management of strategic uncertainties requires an understanding of the key assumptions underlying the strategy and monitoring changes in the business environment to ensure that these assumptions remain valid over time.

2. It is not what we know that matters; it is what we don't know that makes the difference. The question should be: Is our approach to assessing risk identifying emerging risks and telling us something we don't know?

3. Most businesses are boundary-less. A strategic perspective applied to operational risks suggests the need for an end-to-end extended enterprise view of the value chain, requiring consideration of upstream and downstream relationships. What happens if any critical component of this chain were lost for an indeterminate period of time?

4. Sooner or later, there will be a crisis that will test your company. Even the most effective risk

management cannot prevent this exposure. Yet companies spend a lot of time guessing at probabilities and ignoring the speed of impact, the persistence of impact over time and the organization's response readiness.

5. Management and directors are struggling with delineating between risk management and risk oversight. The risk oversight playbook is evolving. CEOs fear an overlay and non-value-added activity that is out of sync with the rhythm of the business.

It makes sense to start both risk management and risk oversight at the same place – with the formulation of strategy, including an understanding of the key assumptions underlying the strategy.

These five realities are forcing management and their boards to take a fresh look at risk and crisis management to plan for the future and also make wise choices.

COSO's Enterprise Risk Management Model

COSO's enterprise risk management (ERM) model has become a widely accepted framework for organizations to use. Although it has attracted criticisms, the framework has been established as a model that can be used in different environments worldwide.

COSO's guidance illustrated the ERM model in the form of a cube. COSO intended the cube to illustrate the links between objectives that are shown on the top and the eight components shown on the front, which represent what is needed to achieve the objectives.

The third dimension represents the organization's units, which portrays the model's ability to focus on parts of the organization as well as the whole.

1. Internal Environment

The internal environment establishes the tone of the organization, influencing risk appetite, attitudes towards risk management and ethical values.

Ultimately, the company's tone is set by the board. An unbalanced board, lacking appropriate technical knowledge and experience, diversity and strong, independent voices is unlikely to set the right tone.

The work directors do in board committees can also make a significant contribution to tone, with the operation of the audit and risk committees being particularly important.

2. Objective Setting

The board should set objectives that support the organization's mission, and which are consistent with its risk appetite.

If the board is to set objectives effectively, it needs to be aware of the risks arising if different objectives are pursued. Entrepreneurial risks are risks that arise from carrying out business activities, such as the risks arising from a major business investment or competitor activities.

The board also needs to consider risk appetite and take a high-level view of how much risk it is willing to accept. Risk tolerance – the acceptable variation around individual objectives – should be aligned with risk appetite.

3. Event Identification

The organization must identify internal and external events that affect the achievement of its objectives.

The COSO guidance draws a distinction between events having a negative impact that represent risks and events having a positive impact that are opportunities, which should feedback to strategy setting.

Some organizations may lack a process for event identification in important areas. There may be a culture of no-one expecting anything to go wrong.

4. Risk Assessment

The likelihood and impact of risks are assessed, as a basis for determining how to manage them.

As well as mapping the likelihood and impact of individual risks, managers also need to consider how individual risks interrelate.

The COSO guidance stresses the importance of employing a combination of qualitative and quantitative risk assessment methodologies. As well as assessing inherent risk levels, the organization should also assess residual risks left after risk management actions have been taken.

The ERM model has, though, been criticized for encouraging an over-simplified approach to risk assessment. It's claimed that it encourages an approach that views the materialization of risk as a single outcome.

This outcome could be an expected outcome, or it could be a worst-case result. Many risks will have a range of possible outcomes if they materialize – for example, extreme weather – and risk assessment needs to consider this range

5. Risk Response

Management selects appropriate actions to align risks with risk tolerance and risk appetite.

This stage can be seen in terms of the four main responses – reduce, accept, transfer or avoid. However, risks may end up being treated in isolation without considering the picture for the organization as a whole.

Portfolio management and diversification will be best implemented at the organizational level and the COSO guidance stresses the importance of taking a portfolio view of risk.

The risk responses chosen must be realistic, taking into account the costs of responding as well as the impact on risk. An organization's environment will affect its risk responses.

Highly regulated organizations, for example, will have more complex risk responses and controls than less regulated organizations.

The ALARP principle – as low as reasonably

practicable – has become important here, particularly in sectors where health or safety risks are potentially serious but are unavoidable.

6. Control Activities

Policies and procedures should operate to ensure that risk responses are effective.

Once designed, the controls in place need to operate properly. COSO has supplemented the ERM model by guidance in 'Internal Control – Integrated Framework'.

The latest draft of this framework was published in December 2011. It stresses that control activities are a means to an end and are affected by people.

The guidance states: 'It is not merely about policy manuals, systems and forms but people at every level of an organization that impact on internal control.'

7. Information and Communication

Information systems should ensure that data is identified, captured and communicated in a format and timeframe that enables managers and staff to carry out their responsibilities.

The information provided to management needs to be relevant and of appropriate quality. It also must cover all the objectives shown on the top of the cube.

There needs to be communication with staff. Communication of risk areas that are relevant to what staff do is an important means of strengthening the internal environment by embedding risk awareness in staff's thinking.

8. Monitoring

The management system should be monitored and modified if necessary. Guidance on monitoring has developed significantly since the initial COSO guidance. At board level, the Turnbull guidance on the scope of regular and annual review of risk management has been very important. COSO supplemented its ERM guidance with specific guidance on monitoring internal controls in 2009, based on the principle that unmonitored controls tend to deteriorate over time.

The guidance echoes the Turnbull guidance in drawing a distinction between regular review (ongoing monitoring) and periodic review (separate evaluation). When weaknesses are identified, they are reported, assessed and their root causes corrected.

How to Start an Orphanage

A Humanitarian

How to Start an Orphanage

This photo brings beautiful memories. it's a team from USA brought in by Apostle Angela Enje Rucker and have supported many children, she has since then become like family to me.

A humanitarian is someone who actively engages in promoting human welfare and social reforms, and who has no prejudice with human suffering on grounds of gender, sexual orientation, religious or national divisions.

A humanitarian's goal is to save lives, relieve suffering, and maintain human dignity. This can be done in the form of rescuing and providing safety for refugees, providing shelter and food for the homeless, or helping people in the aftermath of natural disasters or civil unrest.

Humanitarians battle disease, hunger and violence in some of the most inhospitable situations, locations and climates and they persevere despite the risks of kidnappings, death threats, murder and other deadly and abusive behavior from the communities they work within.

What Does A Humanitarian Do?

Humanitarians promote human welfare and ideas of people; they bring about change in the normal behavioral patterns of a society and help to aid by giving money or necessities for those in need.

Necessities could be in the form of food, water, clothing, shelter, equipment and medical supplies which give relief to people in unfortunate and desperate situations.

Doing and participating in something that results in an act of kindness goes a long way in someone's eyes. The simple act of donating money to a charity or a cause that one believes in is also considered a humanitarian act and should not be measured by how much time or money is spent.

It takes a lot for a person to care about someone they do not personally know. It is a wonderful human ability to be able to understand struggle, loss, pain and fear and to turn that understanding into a humanitarian act. In turn, this brings happiness, not only to the one(s) in need, but to the person giving the helping hand.

At the end of the day, a humanitarian does not look

for glory or praise. His or her main goal is to make a difference in the world they live in, to make someone's life better than what it is, and to ease the plight of people that have little hope.

Humanitarians have distinct personalities. They tend to be social individuals, which means they're kind, generous, cooperative, patient, caring, helpful, empathetic, tactful, and friendly. They excel at socializing, helping others, and teaching. Some of them are also conventional, meaning they're conscientious and conservative.

What is the workplace of a humanitarian like?

The workplace of a humanitarian is not subject to one particular place. It can be anywhere in the world that is in need of help. Whether it is working from a desk in your local community or digging a well in Africa, a humanitarian is someone that acknowledges the importance of forming strong working bonds with their community and other communities.

People from all over the world, from different walks of life and different faiths, can make a difference by their humanitarian acts.

How to Start an Orphanage

Strategic Organization Development

The organization development can be centered on three (3) of the following programs;

1. Mission programs
2. Sponsorship program
3. International volunteering program

Mission Programs

These are programs drawn out of the vision and aimed to equip missionaries as vessels to reach out and give a helping hand. These programs can be to orphanages, schools, pediatric hospitals among others.

Sponsorship Programs

This is aimed towards mobilizing support for less privileged children in order to attain a quality life through education, healthy living and social life. Under the sponsorship program, there are activities which are done to keep connection of sponsors and their children and these include.

- Letter writing
- Bible study/children camps
- Career guidance

International Volunteering Program

They are a great addition towards the development of the organization. Attracting international visitors who are interested in serving with the organization from a period of 2 weeks to a year.

They are an addition alarm of support in aiding day today work to realize the vision of the organization through their involvement in mission programs, sponsoring children and be in ambassadors of the organization across the globe.

How to Realize The 3 Programs

There has got to be an internal and external strategy in order for the organisations to develop and sustain itself in the long run. Here are some ideas that can be easily implemented at different stages and levels.

Internal Strategy

1. **Structured staff team**
    - Team leader (Oversee communication, international relations fore casting the vision among others)
    - Programs/Mission leader
    - Accountant

- International volunteer coordinator
- Head of Sponsorship
- Mission House Chief
- Security guard
- Management

2. **Scheduled mission program activities**

School out reaches, babies' home support, Orphanage ministry, sports outreach, camping mission trips.

External Strategy

1. **Brand identity**
   Redesigning the organization brand and image, logo, social media content and a website
2. Contacting international friends of good will for support in organizing speaking engagements in mainly: -

   - Churches (especially with mission departments)
   - University/colleges/ High school
3. Organization Ambassadors.

They are Creating partnerships with organizations and churches that can stand with the organization.

Conclusion

How to Start an Orphanage

This is the right time for all those interested in humanitarian work to start helping these children to get education through a Nonprofit, Government scheme or self-sponsoring (if you have capacity of that) so that they can get a bright future and fulfill their aspirations. Its giving humanity a second chance to becoming a somebody.

There are many ways you and I can contribute to the wellbeing of these children in our continent. There are many ways of sponsorship programs like, providing necessities of food, clothing, shoes, shelter, medical care, schoolbooks, school supplies, education and much more. Africa is one of the best countries in the world and the kind of work we do is truly needed to make the world a better place.

Many of these children are hungry, neglected, abused, and or abandoned. The people of Africa, however, are beautiful, friendly, and inviting of our assistance. This book has provided you with a wide array of programs that will benefit the children and the community.

Starting an orphanage in Africa will make a genuine difference in the lives of orphans. It will ensure they get what they need to thrive! Let us help empower children without parents.

How to Start an Orphanage

We at Blessed Hill are now moving to the next stage and trusting God for divine helpers and partnerships.

- Building more infrastructure. At the moment there are only primary and nursery school facilities and are looking to expand to having more buildings like ,a vocational school where the children who finish primary 7 and are ready to go to secondary but can't continue because of lack of sponsorship can come to the vocation and learn some life skills like baking, carpentry and woodwork, tailoring/ textile and clothing, brick making, catering and cookery which can help them survive on their own when they return to their communities.
- Construction of staff quarters or houses and guest house for the volunteers and for those who look after the children.
- Building a health facility/ Community dispensary to treat the children who fall sick but also to extend health services to the community since we have spotted it as a big challenge in our nearby community.
- Buying land dedicated to growing our own in-house food to feed the staff and children as the children learn agriculture too.
- Creating a computer lab with computers to

teach the children IT skills.

Thanks for taking your time to read through this book, I hope you will take a step of faith and do that which God has ordained you to do!

Life Is Too Short to Live Someone Else's Dream. Chase Your Dreams, it is possible for them to manifest.

About the Author

Mrs. Lucy Sabiiti is the founder of Blessed Hill Nursery and Primary School which is home to hundreds of orphans from across the country of Uganda. She is a mother of many and has a desire to help children.

For more information contact me at:

- Email: lucysabiitifoundation@gmail.com
- You Tube: Lucy Sabiiti Foundation
- Facebook: Blessed Hill Children's Centre

How to Start an Orphanage

www.ingramcontent.com/pod-product-compliance
Lightning Source LLC
Chambersburg PA
CBHW042336150426
43195CB00001B/8